ROCKSTAR PRINCIPLES

Teen's *for* Happiness

THE GREATNESS GUIDE FOR TEENAGERS

Paramjit Kaur

CO AUTHOR ANDAL KRISHNAN

PARTRIDGE

A Penguin Random House Company

Library of Congress Control Number:		2014940464
ISBN:	Hardcover	978-1-4828-9960-3
	Softcover	978-1-4828-9959-7
	eBook	978-1-4828-9975-7

To order additional copies of this book, contact
Toll Free 800 101 2657 (Singapore)
Toll Free 1 800 81 7340 (Malaysia)
orders.singapore@partridgepublishing.com

www.partridgepublishing.com/singapore

May you receive all the Joy and Happiness.

It is your Birthright.

This is our prayer for you and all the teenagers of this world.

Paramjit Kaur and Andal Krishnan

"You are the creator of your own destiny. No one else creates problems, miseries or pains for you, not even God. God is the center of equality and love, so why should God be partial?

Why should God make one person happy and another unhappy? That doesn't make any sense; whatever human beings experience, they think it is the result of God's will, but God does not make anyone unhappy.

Happiness or unhappiness is of your own creation. To live is a gift, but to live happily is of your own making."

Swami Rama—The Art of Joyful Lving

Contents

Authors' Preface

The one belief that propelled us to work on this book is that no teenager should ever experience unhappiness because happiness is their birthright.

Our teenagers are our responsibility because they are our future generation.

The life changing principles in this book are no invention of ours; they are universal principles from various sacred scriptures of our Divine Universe and the wisdom from many other written sources and also, our own years of experience and observation, based on the success of others around us.

We do not take credit entirely for the development of this book as it was written in collaboration with parents, teachers and teenagers. Our deepest gratitude to them, for sharing their thoughts so willingly.

The book is written in a conversational style as we have used the language of oral communication. The reader friendliness of the book will hopefully create a bond between the book and the reader, encourage several readings and become a reference point in the journey of life for teenagers and their well wishers.

Whenever there is a divine undertaking, our lives are orchestrated by our loving Guardian Angels, Masters of Divine

Light and Love, and Divine Invisible Spiritual Guides and Teachers. Therefore we record our deepest gratitude to these Loving Beings for their help and guidance.

And most importantly our deepest gratitude to God, the ultimate source of our Happiness. All gifts that exist around us are presented to us by our Most Loving, Kind, and the All-Mighty Divine God.

Author   Co-Author
ParamjitKaur   Andal Krishnan

PROLOGUE

Joy . . . . Happiness. All good Things in Life Are Your Birthright

We are born to be happy. That is our true state.

However, in reality, we start becoming anxious and lack optimism even at an early age.

That is not right and we need to reclaim our right to be happy.

When you are a teenager, you struggle to learn about your personality. It can be confusing to realize who you truly are and what you want to be, when everyone expects you to act in a certain way and this can lead to frustration and unhappiness.

You might try to fix these feelings by engaging in reckless behaviour. Or you may feel weighed down by fears of the future such as exams, recession, peer pressure, family pressure . . . You are faced with awkward questions such as . . . Will I do well at school? Are my career decisions the right one?

Relationship matters . . . Habits need to be changed/developed . . . . So many issues need to be resolved.

During times of conflicts, you feel terrible things are happening to you; you wonder why life is painful. Your self-esteem dwindles within this turbulence. You feel lethargic and useless.

However there is an antidote. And that is to abide by the Rockstar Principles of Happiness with which we can overcome the uncertainties of life, reap success and lead a harmonious life in a state of happiness.

The Rockstar principles of happiness will help keep you safe and at peace while you develop your adult character.

Ask yourself:

❖ *Do I need happiness?*
❖ *Do I want to be healthier?*
❖ *Do I wish to enjoy life even more?*

If your answer is "yes" to any of these questions, then this book can help you reach a secure state of mind, and maintain a fulfilling life and perfect health while succeeding in all your endeavours.

No doubt your happiness is your birthright. But you have to claim this state of being. The choice to be happy has to be made by you.

Once you have said to yourself that I want to and will be happy, the prescription in this book performs magic and the transformation begins.

You will wonder how your thinking have taken a new perspective of the events around you.

You will be in awe of the miracles that happen in your environment.

You will start to understand the control that you have in your destiny.

You will become the magnet of good things and great people.

Take the first step . . . Read this book . . . . Experience a whole new world.

CHAPTER 1

YOU ARE A GIFT
YOUR LIFE IS A GIFT

"Live your life while you have it. Life is a splendid gift."

Florence Nightingale

YOU ARE A GIFT
YOUR LIFE IS A GIFT

Your life deserves to be celebrated

Although there are many answers to the eternal question of WHO AM I, the most important answer you will find is YOU ARE A GIFT of this DIVINE UNIVERSE and your LIFE IS A GIFT that deserves to be celebrated.

You are a special child of our Divine Universe. Your life is too beautiful and precious. Your life is meant to be filled with abundant of joy and happiness. This is your birthright.

Observe the wisdom of Marelin the Magician in his book *Merlin's Message* "You are extremely important in the evolution of all that is. You are worthy, simply because you are."

You are a beautiful creation of God, as magnificent as any of God's creations! You have a divine purpose in this! You're here to shine, to accomplish, celebrate life, and celebrate your sacred purpose!

Honour and cherish yourself for what you are, who you are, and what you have.

Give yourself appreciation — just as you appreciate a butterfly's delicate beauty, or a mountain's grandeur.

Honour your Authenticity. It is a gift

It is human nature to compare ourselves with others. Often we do it without really thinking about it. This is an unhealthy habit that you should make an effort to curtail. When you negatively compare yourself to others, you dishonour your own authenticity, which is a Divine Gift from God.

Sean Covey, in his book 7 *Habits of Highly Effective Teenagers* said "Comparing is Competition's twin. And just as cancerous. Comparing yourself to others is nothing but bad news. Why? We are all in different development timetables—socially, mentally, and physically."

Comparing your looks to those of others will only make you insecure and self-conscious. Just look around you. Your friends and classmates come in different body shapes and colours and sizes. Everyone is different and unique.

So, why stress yourself trying to meet some imaginary expectations concocted by the media? The media's presentation of "good looks" is artificial and based on fantasy, not reality. If you truly want to feel and look beautiful, just take a look at yourself in the mirror. Look at your features and the way that you like to style your hair. Look at your clothing and the way *you* like to wear it.

Be amazed at the fascinating elements of your body. Be amazed at its intelligence, and its ability to react to life. Your body is even able to heal your physical wounds, infection and pain.

Appreciate your body. It is magnificent and you will realize how flawlessly it has been designed. Your body has great strength and regenerative capabilities. And it can function independently with little guidance from you.

Look at the uniqueness of your facial features, eye colour, hair and everything, **you are truly beautiful.** You are not meant to be carbon copies of anyone. Your authenticity makes you a unique gem.

Television shows, films and songs tell you that life should be exciting and romantic, you should be attractive and sexy and you should have all the latest clothes and gadgets to become the perfect person.

This isn't real life. And you know it isn't. But it is easy to get sucked into the myth, and believe that you will magically become more attractive or popular if you wear a certain brand of clothing or have the latest iPhone.

The issue becomes more confusing when celebrities and role models who are viewed as being "perfect" have used unnatural methods to change themselves in order to become perfect. Some used plastic surgery. Everybody has an opinion of themselves. You should be happy with your appearance and personality.

Being a teenager, you are also always worrying about how you look. Your body is changing so it suddenly doesn't seem familiar to you any more—it's hard to maintain a strong self-esteem when you don't recognize the person in the mirror!

When you are self-conscious about your looks, it is easy to assume other people are secretly critical of you. You're always wondering what other people think about you so you might be tempted to change yourself to win their approval. This is a normal part of growing up, while you learn about who you are and what is important to you.

You have your own beautiful authentic style. Don't be too hard on yourself by wanting to be like somebody else. Legendary actress Judy Garland once said, "Always be a first-rate version of yourself, instead of a second—rate version of somebody else."

Ask yourself:

❖ *What is important to me?*
❖ *What clothes make me feel happiest and most comfortable?*

Your answers may not fit the latest trends but you will have a greater sense of your own authentic personality. Just like not everyone has the same taste for food, not everyone will like the same style of clothes. Others can give you suggestions or ideas on what to wear but in the end, the opinion that matters the most has to be yours.

Smile confidently at yourself and recognize the potential shining from within you. You are unique, with so much to offer and so much to experience and enjoy. And you are more precious and beautiful than you think.

God made you special. He gave you many beautiful features and qualities. All of these things together are what make you unique. When God created you, God already had in mind the marvellous things you would be able to accomplish with your life. Think about the talents you have. **Thank God** for those and then ask how you can use those talents to become what you dream of being.

Don't look at yourself and say "I want to change myself."

Ask yourself, "Do I look healthy?"

Your health has a strong effect on your appearance and your nutrition has a strong effect on your health. So if your skin is blotchy, your hair is lank and oily and you seem either underweight or overweight, examine your diet. You might find that by incorporating more fresh food into your diet, you will look, feel healthier and your looks will improve.

When you are not happy with your appearance, concentrate on streamlining rather than changing your appearance. Work with your natural look by experimenting with your hair and trying different styles of clothing until you pinpoint exactly what suits you best.

When you learn how to look your best naturally, you will not be so inclined to compare yourself to others. And you will honour your authenticity.

With a nice smile say to yourself:

"I am God's Divine Offspring. I love myself, I love my authenticity. I love the way I look, talk, smile and laugh. I am God's gift and my life is a Gift and Blessing."

CHAPTER 2

YOUR MIND HAS AMAZING POWERS

"Everything is based on mind, is led by mind,
is fashioned by mind. If you speak and act with a
polluted mind, suffering will follow. If you speak and
act with a pure mind, happiness will follow you."

Buddha

YOUR MIND
HAS AMAZING POWERS

You become what you think.
So! Become a powerful thinker

The most important tool for our happiness and health is our own mental power. Our mind consistently generates powerful energy that affects our body and our life alike.

"You become what you think" is a powerful saying that claims, our happiness and unhappiness stems from our own mind. But some of us know very little about the tremendous powers of our mind, or how it works.

Your mind is a force powered by your thoughts. And since your mind is made up of a collection of thoughts, it is extremely powerful. This is because the ideas that you have in your mind often become reality once they are carried out. Ponder on the wisdom of British philosophical writer James Allen "You are today where your thoughts have brought you; you will be tomorrow where your thoughts take you."

Just imagine . . . **"Thoughts"** created everything around you. The creation of every palace, every building, and every piece of technology first began with, "thought."

German Physicist, Albert Einstein beautifully said "The world we have created is a product of our thinking; it cannot be changed without changing our thinking."

Think of your brain as a radio station. Suddenly, someone walks by and you have a thought about that person.

Is it possible that your thought—which is generated almost like a radio wave in your brain—can be picked up by the other person? Whatever the case may be, it's possible that you can receive the thoughts of others without even realizing it.

Thoughts are like magnets. Some people believe that thoughts are like magnets. Whenever you dwell upon something, it seems to come true. Maybe you were just thinking of someone seconds before they walked through the door.

Or perhaps you were thinking about calling someone just as your phone begins to ring, and it is the same person you were just planning to call. In a way your thoughts are like a magnet.

Positive Thoughts versus Negative Thoughts. Have you ever noticed that negative thoughts seem to attract negative actions? If you store only negative thoughts in your mind, negative actions will occur. However, if you think positive, your actions become positive.

Have you ever had one of those days when everything seems to go wrong?

You could tell yourself that everyone and everything is against you, or you could look back rationally and see how your negative thoughts have triggered accidents and misunderstandings.

Perhaps you slept in late and you were cross while you rushed to get dressed and accidentally yanked off a shirt button.

Sometimes your negative thoughts can cause more damage than a lost button. When you have a negative response to your responsibilities, such as homework, you will always have the weight of anxiety hanging over you. This weighty anxiety will loom large even while you enjoy yourself reading magazines or playing video games, as you are constantly aware that you are supposed to be doing your homework.

When you do your homework promptly, you can relax completely afterwards as you read magazines or watch television. You will feel happier and more confident at school and you will find the time to do other enjoyable and other rewarding activities.

However when you are positive, your actions become positive, you become happy and confident. You are more likely to do nice things for others. If you help an elderly lady to cross the street or guide a lost child back to his mother, these positive actions will inspire positive thoughts in other people, who appreciate your kindness.

Thoughts are full of energy. They will always influence you, your life, and the lives of those around you. If you constantly give in to negative thinking, your life will be in a negative mode. If you think positively, you are bound to live a life of happiness and positive achievement.

How to Make Your Negative Thoughts Disappear

To have a happy life you must remove negative thoughts from your mind. One simple way to get rid of bad thoughts is by the Drain and Fill Method. This method trains you to eliminate negative thoughts and focus on thinking positively.

The Drain and Fill Method. With the Drain and Fill Method you replace your negative thoughts with the positive counterpart. Imagine yourself "drinking" your thoughts from your mind, just as you would drink from a clear glass. If you did not like the taste of the juice in the glass, what do you do? You would pour the juice down the drain. Once you get rid of the unpleasant juice, you replace it with a drink that you do like.

When your mind begins to fill with negative thoughts, all you need to do is empty your mind of everything that you do not like, and refill it with positive and happy thoughts. For example, rather than saying, *"I will never pass that exam—it is too hard,"* you should ask yourself: *"What can I do to improve my chances of passing the exam?"*

When you think positively, you have a plan of action and an optimistic outlook. By working out what to do next, you also regain a sense of control over a challenging situation.

Positive thoughts attract positive results. While negative thoughts only make the situation worse. Rather than dwell on the bad thoughts, it is better to drain them from your mind and replace them with good thoughts and positive actions. And being aware of your thoughts and practicing having positive thoughts can help you have more positive things happen and this always help you look at life with a better frame of mind.

Become a Deliberate Creator

Marelin the Magician in his handbook *Merlin's Message* said "Others cannot create for you or make you feel anything. Others can influence you but you are ultimately in creative control. Since your thoughts determine your experience, be deliberate in choosing them. Look at the word "liberate" within deliberate. You are liberated to experience your full potential when you deliberately think thoughts." Perfect point!

When you see a dedicated athlete at work, either training or competing, you can see the benefit of deliberately focussing on positive thought patterns.

How can someone become an elite athlete if they gave up when the training seemed "too hard" or the desired result seemed too far in the distance?

Imagining Success. Elite athletes train their minds as diligently as they train their bodies by deliberately visualizing the final victory; their self-talk is positive, powerful and in alignment with their desires. Elite athletes don't let anything pollute their vision and they master their minds the same way they master their bodies.

Legendary father of modern psychology William James gave a powerful statement "There is a law in psychology that if you form a picture in your mind of what you would like to be, and you keep and hold that picture there long enough, you will soon become exactly as you have been thinking." Amazing wisdom!

Whatever you desire, imagine it deeply. Savour the image of your final result and savour all the emotions you experience as you work towards the success of your goal. Continue imagining the success while you work to master the next step. Then, watch what happens.

Remember, there must be no doubts, only faith, and often say to yourself: "*I deserve success and all the good things in life, as it is my birthright.*"

Become a deliberate creator of your life by monitoring and discriminating your thoughts, having inner positive dialogue and imagination. Every persistent thought and inner dialogue attracts another and another.

Deliberately replace all negative thoughts. You are not at the mercy of any external forces. God has blessed you with the ability to master your mind. **Use that gift!**

Get Motivated

If you want to achieve something, you have to give yourself a reason to reach your goal. Set a target, and go after it 150%. The target will serve as a positive reason for you to keep pushing towards your goal.

If your target is too far in the future, set a few smaller targets so you can boost your confidence with a series of small successes along the way.

An elite athlete doesn't begin by winning an Olympic medal — he trains every day, he masters the local races, the national championships and has wide experience in international events before reaching the final goal.

There is more to success than simply daydreaming about what you want—ask yourself: *"What do I need to do to achieve this? What should I do right now?"*

Change your thinking pattern

There is one phrase that is guaranteed to trigger discouragement and failure: *"I can't . . ."* So what is the antidote to this poisonous, confidence-sapping phrase?

Ask: *"How can I . . ." or "What can I do instead?"* Rather than stopping short at the *"I can't"* moment, think around the obstacle so you can find your way around it or plot a different course.

This thinking pattern helps you stay control of your destiny as well as opening new avenues for success and positive experience.

American writer Dale Carnegie said "Remember happiness doesn't depend upon who you are or what you have; it depends solely upon what you think."

Be with people who think positively

Negativity is contagious, and so is laziness. Some people are negative, simply because it saves them the effort of trying to succeed. If you constantly hang out with pessimistic friends, it will affect the way you think and view life.

Take heed of this wisdom from the book *Be Extraordinary: The Greatness Guide Book Two* authored by Robin Sharma "Invite people into your professional life and personal life who inspire you. Who will uplift you. Who will make you more extraordinary/ authentic/unforgettable (and loving). Who are viscerally committed to world class. And, most importantly, who see the world through a different set of eyes. They'll challenge you. They'll push you. And sometimes maybe they'll even irritate you (if so, fantastic). This practice will serve you well. So that you grow. And reach. And evolve. So that you will never be the same."

Wow! What a powerful statement!

When you surround yourself with positive thinkers, you can reinforce your own positive thinking and you will be more motivated to achieve your goal. Besides, confident and positive friends will be happy to cheer you along and congratulate you upon your achievements, as well as boost your spirits when you are feeling discouraged.

Transform your positive thoughts into positive actions!

Think of how great you will feel when you have finally completed your goal. Think about all of the benefits and the positive results you will enjoy when you achieved your task. Focusing on your future sense of achievement will help you stay disciplined. It will allow you to do all of the things that you set out to do.

Take your destiny to the next level by transforming positive thoughts into positive actions. After all, being positive is not only reflected in how you think but it is also most strongly reflected in what you do positively.

There are two important elements to creating a positive action. Follow through, and finish. If you say you will do something, make sure you follow through and actually do it. And always make sure you finish what you start.

With a smile, say to yourself:

"From this moment onwards, I will pay more attention to all of my thoughts. I will separate the negative ones from the good, and only accept thoughts that bring me happiness and a sense of purpose. I make a conscious decision that every thought, every word, every story, every belief, every feeling, every imagination, and visualization that I have makes me feel strong and positive at all times. I release negative thoughts that no longer serve me right now."

You are Stronger than the Enemy Called FEAR

How many wonderful dreams never flower into achievement because of fear! Fear is the most destructive negative energy of all human emotions. Some of us have been literally paralyzed into inaction by fear. We let fear dictate our lives . . . but it doesn't have to be this way! We can overcome fear, achieve our dreams and live a happy life. Here is how.

There is 'positive' fear which alerts us to danger, and prompts a survival response.

There is also 'negative' fear, when we are so terrified that we cannot drum up the courage to step forward in our lives. This is the fear of "what if". This is the destroyer of dreams. This negative fear is an ILLUSION, merely a representation of how we view life.

Based on this fact, fear has even developed into a catchy acronym: False Evidence Appearing Real.

How to drive out fear

One way of handling fear is confrontation. If fear is holding you back, you need to investigate what happened to make you instinctively avoid danger in certain situations.

For example, perhaps you are terrified of speaking in front of the class because you were once embarrassed when you were poorly prepared and everybody laughed at you. Rather than avoiding public speaking, prepare your speech carefully and practice it until you know it by heart.

Confront your fear rather than avoiding it and you will feel a greater sense of achievement and be able to move on with your life.

Every time you find yourself saying *"what if"* or *"what if I fail."* Replace it with **"I can" and "I will"**, and back them up with a strong, determined posture, commanding attitude and bold action.

This strategy is extremely empowering. The more practice you have at driving out the *"what ifs"*, the more you will see that it holds no power over you.

Be a Super Hero of Optimism

Life can have twists and turns which make things difficult and sometimes it can be really hard to see how things can improve.

I am sure you have heard the saying: **"Every cloud has a silver lining."**

You should always look on the bright side of life. Believe that it will get better in the future. This way of looking at things will always make you feel as though better things are right around the corner.

You may have had something happen that has knocked you down. But you know that you need to get back up again. Thinking about how you want things to be in the future will help you to focus more on the present.

Say to yourself, **"Right now, I want to be happy."** That way, your mind-set will begin to change and you will be on the road to happiness.

Focus on what is going on in your life right now. Make sure you are not dwelling on bad things that happened in the past. If you regret something that you did in the past, don't sit and sulk about it. Learn from it so that you won't make the same mistake! And then, move on.

If you dwell on negative things from the "past", they will eventually find their way into your "present", and stick around until they reach your "future".

Believing in yourself. When everything else seems as though it has failed, just believe in yourself. Believing in yourself will give you the strength and courage to face your fears, and fix your problems. It will help you take control of your life and decide how your life story will improve.

Imagine that you are the creator of a film. You get to write the plot and decide how the storyline will twist and turn, and how the film will end.

Often say to yourself, *"I have the power to do anything with my life that I choose to do."*

More than anything, you need to trust yourself more. You need to be confident, think positively and get rid of all the nasty and negative thoughts that may have crept into your mind. If you do have something negative that you need to overcome, be constructive about it. Be realistic and think of ways to solve it so that you can improve.

Sometimes things may go wrong. But if you can see the bright side to your problems, you eventually learn to move on. The past does matter, but the now and the future are more important to living a happy life.

Legendary Prime Minister of the United Kingdom (1940 to 1945) Sir Winston Churchill once said "A pessimist sees the difficulty in every opportunity; an optimist sees the opportunity in every difficulty." Superb Wisdom!

With a smile say to yourself:

"I will see all challenges as an opportunity for me to grow and strengthen my character."

CHAPTER 3

BE A ROCKSTAR OF EMOTIONS

*"I have learned silence from the talkative,
toleration from the intolerant, and kindness
from the unkind; yet strange,
I am grateful to those teachers."*

Kahlil Gibran

BE A ROCKSTAR
OF EMOTIONS

Chill! Dont let your emotions get the best of you

*Y*our emotions make you human and individual. Do you cry at movies? Do you have a quirky sense of humour?

This is you, the person you are, and the person your life has shaped you to become. You need to be at peace with your natural emotional responses, but you also need to let go of unnecessary negative emotions. Your emotional state can directly and indirectly affect your physical health.

Feelings of anger, depression, resentment, loneliness, bitterness, jealousy, frustration, hatred, grief and pessimism are all natural emotions that affect everybody at some time. It can be challenging to deal with these negative emotions in a healthy and constructive manner.

Do you suppress your negative feelings, thinking you have to appear "happy" and "good" all the time?

Or do you feel entitled to lash out into a destructive tantrum as soon as things go against you?

Or do you retreat into a dark and lonely place to brood about how nobody likes you or nothing goes right for you?

These emotions are linked to some problems for people in general. So, don't let these emotions get the best of you.

Cooling your Anger

Anger is the natural human emotion. If anger is not controlled; it can cause people to lash out and sometimes cause harm to others. This is why we are socially conditioned to suppress our anger rather than expressing it. Suppressing anger is also dangerous, as the emotion must leak out in some way.

Imagine that your anger was a blanket and you needed to cram it into a cardboard box so nobody sees it. You keep cramming more blankets into the box until finally the sides of the box start to break. Rather than keeping these "**blankets**" hidden, you need to air them out so they can be useful and practical.

However, there is no harm in suppressing your anger for a short while, simply so you can think the situation through before you say something.

What if your friends make a joke that you found hurtful?

Do you lash out and tell them how rude they are? Or do you keep your mouth shut, even though you have lost your trust in your friends because of their hurtful joke?

The best option is somewhere in the middle: think about the incident quietly to yourself and ask yourself:

❖ *Did they really mean to hurt my feelings?*
❖ *If not, should they have realized that they were saying something hurtful?*

❖ *Can I let this go?*

If the incident still bothers and irritates you, take the powerful wisdom of the famous psychologist Carl Jung: "Everything that irritates us about others can lead us to an understanding of ourselves."

Robin Sharma in his book *The Greatness Guide* penned a powerful point. "The things that irritate, annoy and anger you are entry points into your evolution and elevation as a human being. They are signposts for what you need to work on and fears you need to face. They are gifts of growth."

If you are angry, don't bury your natural feelings, however, don't feel entitled to hit someone or smash something.

Take a deep breath and say in a calm, strong voice:

*"I am angry about this because . . . **but I must remain calm."***

Just articulating why you are angry can help you make sense of the situation; and who knows? The person who angered you might offer a solution or apologize! If not, at least he/she realizes you won't accept being treated badly.

It is always best to take some time to consider why you are angry before you deal directly with the situation. If you feel a sudden rush of anger in response to a difficult situation, you might say something thoughtless and inappropriate that makes the situation worse — or you might do something physically violent.

The best strategy for curbing anger is to **"count 1 to 25"** before speaking.

Everyone gets angry at one time or another. The way you handle that anger is what defines your character. And the way people, especially those who look up to you, view you. Sometimes they want to do things you do so they can be like you.

Deal with the things that make you angry in a positive and calm way. In this manner, you are showing those who look UP to you as a role model that it's okay to get angry, but there are better ways to handle it than losing your temper.

One most powerful method to overcome anger is take heed of this powerful wisdom from Famous Author William Arthur Ward "It is wise to direct your anger towards problems—not people; to focus your energies on answers—not excuses."

Managing Depression

It is not unusual to feel a little low occasionally. Sometimes you may feel upset because you feel left out, or you feel unsatisfied with the way your life is going. But everybody has experienced this at one point or another. This mood usually occurs when you need to shake your life up a bit and find a new direction.

However, when you feel depressed, you are too low to find a new direction for your life; in fact, you might not be able to pinpoint exactly what is wrong with your life. Perhaps you have been suppressing emotions such as anger, so now you have trouble identifying your true emotions.

Instead, you only feel a dark sense of depression and hopelessness.

Those closest to you may not understand exactly how you are feeling, or recognize the problem for exactly what it is.

It's good to spend some time by yourself every once in a while; it's good to have **"alone time"** to think things through a little. But you can't be alone for too long. Talk to your friends, your parents, or teachers. Or talk to someone you are comfortable with or you can trust or seek a professional therapist for counselling sessions. By talking to someone, you might discover the real problem lying deep in your mind, and you will find a way to handle it.

Depression is like a black hole and it can pull you in deeper and deeper if you try to deal with it alone. *No matter what you do, just remember that you don't have to go through it alone.*

If you have been bullied or abused it is not your fault. You have to tell the truth to the world so that the offender or the criminal does not escape.

It is also therapeutic to try taking control of your life in order to lift your depression. Ask yourself what you are unhappy about—for example, "I'm lonely, I have no friends"—and find a way to actively solve the problem. If you are lonely, try meeting positive minded people or join organisations and associations that will help you develop strength and confidence.

In a different social environment, you might feel freer to be yourself so it is easier to make friends. A new interest will also give you something new to concentrate on, so you are distracted from your dark thoughts.

Remember you are a gift and your life is a gift. Happiness, joy and all the good things in life is your birthright!

Take heed the wisdom of Agatha Christie "I like living. I have sometimes been wildly, despairingly, acutely miserable, racked with sorrow, but through it all I still know quite certainly that just to be alive is a grand thing."

Releasing Worry and Stress

Ever have a big test that you were afraid of failing? You studied and studied but still worry that you will fail. When the teacher finally graded the tests, you learned that you did really well.

All of that worrying and stress was pointless because, in the end, you did just fine. It's important to understand that worrying can affect your mental, physical and emotional health.

Address and categorize your worries: Medical experts have revealed that thinking about what is bothering you can help change the way you view your worries. It can help you learn to deal with them better. The key is to learn how to address your worries before they magnify into stress.

Put your worries into categories: one category for those that can be solved right away and another for those that cannot be fixed.

This way, you will learn to accept that some things are beyond your control, so you can throw those worries away. Then, you can focus your energy on the problems that can be solved or controlled.

Rather than worrying about the test, study for an extra half-hour, so when you catch yourself worrying again, you remember that you are studying hard.

Take care of yourself: Use a range of techniques to relax. Watch a good movie or read a good book. Take time to take care of yourself and take a break from the stress in your life. You can even take up therapeutic exercises such as yoga, stretching or meditation. This will help you relieve some of the stress from your body.

Talk about it: Have a chat with someone who cares about you and can help you to get some perspective on the challenges that you are having. Your friends may have ideas that you might not have thought of. Maybe they can give you some new advice that you can trust, and help you view your situation in a more positive manner.

Finally take note of this wisdom from Founder of Ford Motor Company Legendary Henry Ford. "With God in charge, I believe everything will work out for the best in the end. So what is there to worry about?"

Releasing Anxiety

When worrying becomes a regular habit, it is called Anxiety. Anxiety can affect your emotions and your ability to cope with life and life's stress. It can even make you feel sick, give you headaches, or cause your stomach to feel ill.

Anxiety can cause a number of eating disorders and force your body to have a natural reaction to stress. This is why it is important to learn how to deal with it.

Sometimes we feel anxious because we have taken on too many responsibilities; in this case, you might need to talk to someone about delegating or postponing some of the responsibilities. If you have been sick, your teacher won't expect you to hand your assignment in on the exact day it is due, so ask for an extension.

Stay Healthy—Stick to a healthy diet and make sure you eat regularly. Sleep for around eight hours a night—but if you find yourself lying awake and worrying in the dark, turn on the light and read for a while. Keep your sleep patterns regular by going to bed around the same time every night.

Put things in perspective—Be sure to put the events that stress you out into perspective. Ask yourself the following questions:

- ❖ *What am I really anxious about?*
- ❖ *Are these things really stressing me out?*
- ❖ *So what's the worst thing that can happen?*
- ❖ *Or, If I don't get picked for the team, what would I like to do instead?*
- ❖ *Will I even care about this tomorrow . . . or next week?*

Sometimes, we stress out because it seems like the appropriate response to whatever is happening. Sometimes, there actually is a reason to stress out. In this case, you need to stay cool so you can stay one step ahead of the situation and remain in control. But other times, there is no real reason to be anxious.

Spend time in Nature—One of the things you should do to release anxiety is feast your eyes on the richness and order of nature, its panoramic beauty, the changing scenery of the weather, the enchanting sunrise, the exquisite sunset, multiple shades of the sky; highs and low tides of sea and rivers and the various hues of flora and foliage.

The scents from these natural sources are soothing, healing, and uplifting. Just being in the midst of this beauty sparks an uplift of new energy and peace.

Robin Sharma in his book *Life Lessons from the Monk who sold his Ferrari* said, "While you spend time enjoying nature, observe your surroundings with deep concentration. Study the complexity of a flower or the way the current moves in a sparkling stream. Take your shoes off and feel the grass under your feet. Give silent thanks that you have the privilege of enjoying these special gifts of nature."

Get into physical activity—Another strategy is to plunge into physical activity—swim laps or walk briskly to "out-race" your tension. Not only will this give you a sense of energy and purpose to counteract your worry, stress, anxiety, you will also sleep more soundly at night, helping to restore your equilibrium.

Walter M. Bortz II MD in this book *The Road to 100* said "Movement is life. The absence of movement is the absence of life. Movement should never be thought of as a chore but as an opportunity. Our ability to move is a measure of our mastery of the space we inhibit. It is a marvelous gift. Revel it."

Be an Angel of Sweet Forgiveness

When you forgive someone, it means you no longer want to see them punished for the wrong they did to you. Perhaps you were bullied at school or perhaps one of your friends was disloyal or hurtful. It is natural to want to see the perpetrator punished in some way. And sometimes this will happen . . . Sometimes it won't.

Forgiveness is about you not letting the situation bother you any longer; it really is not about making it better for the person who harmed or hurt you.

But some of us don't like to forgive, and we let our emotions build up inside of us. We focus our energy on negative things such as anger, vengeance, resentment, bitterness and hostility. And eventually, our inability to forgive affects us physically and emotionally, blocking the flow of happiness.

Sports Psychologist Thomas Tulko (B. 1932) beautifully said "Your emotions affect every cell in your body. Mind and body, mental and physical, are interwined." PLEASE THINK ABOUT THIS. IT IS VERY IMPORTANT.

Holding a grudge can be very bad for our health in the long term. When you forgive, you are allowing yourself to forget a painful episode. The person who hurt you no longer has any power over you, because you are no longer allowing them into your mind. And getting rid of all negative thoughts shows these hurtful people, that you are a strong person and beyond their power.

When you choose not to consider forgiveness, you might choose the alternative of vengeance. If you discover that someone stole your backpack, do you steal their backpack in response?

If your friend accidentally broke your mobile phone, would you intentionally break theirs in response? Probably not. That course of action would not fix the fact that *you* don't have a phone. So forgiving is the only answer.

Don't be too hard on yourself.
Forgive yourself

Some of us are prisoners of bitter anger, hurtful memories and are driven by our past guilt and past regrets. We beat ourselves up with blame, and allow it to control our happiness.

If you carry guilt about something that you have done, make a decision to forgive yourself. Mistakes happen in life and it is important to let them go. You can certainly learn from your mistakes so that you won't find yourself in the same situation again.

Do not allow your past unpleasant memories to control your present life and happiness. **Release your past through forgiving yourself.**

Novelist C. Joy Bell said "I have learned, that the person I have to ask for forgiveness from the most is: myself. You must love yourself. You have to forgive yourself, every day, whenever you remember a shortcoming, a flaw; you have to tell yourself "That's just fine". You have to forgive yourself so much, until you don't even see those things anymore."

So forgive others and yourself, and with a sweet smile say:

"I acknowledge that I made a mistake in my past and now that I have learned from my mistakes. I forgive myself and I forgive others."

Have more Laughter in your life

Big Question: When was the last time you had a good laugh? Stress, worry, depression and anger can weigh down our everyday lives so we forget to laugh.

Know that the most wasted days of yours are those in which you have not laughed. Incorporate plenty of laughter every day. Laughter is the most therapeutic remedy for many ailments, and you'll never need a prescription for it, or have to pay for it. You have an unlimited supply of laughter within yourself, and it will almost always make you feel better within seconds.

Laughing and smiling a little each day can make our lives seem more worthwhile. It can make us better people. Laughter is infectious, and spreads joy to others. Sometimes, it's the only cure that actually works.

It has been said that to start his day, Famous Comedian Steve Martin would laugh for five minutes in front of his mirror every morning. Why don't you, instead of getting stressed, worried, depressed or angry, start your day with laughing for few minutes.

However, there is one rule—never laugh *at* someone. Don't use humour to ridicule or undermine another person. If you poison the gift of laughter, you will destroy its beneficial qualities.

Count your Blessings and be Grateful

We live in a material world, when we are constantly bombarded by advertising encouraging us to want *more*, the *best* and the *latest*. When we are sucked into this culture, we are constantly dissatisfied because we are being brainwashed into concentrating on what we don't have.

A Greek Sage—Epictetus (AD55-135) said "He is a wise man who does not grieve for the things which he has not, but rejoices for those which he has."

So, count your blessings and be grateful. Focus on what you *do* have and not what you don't have.

Discipline yourself to avoid the modern trap of consumerism — just because your friend has the latest phone doesn't mean you are suddenly deprived. You may suddenly find yourself looking at your classmates and feeling a sense of jealousy because they have something that you don't have.

Don't judge yourself by your own possessions; otherwise you will never measure up; because there is always a new gadget, a new designer label and a new trend. You'll never keep up and if you feel that you have to, you will never be content.

Eventually, your desires may grow so much that you always want to have the new version of everything. You will end up spending all of your money.

Rather than worrying about what you have or don't have, think about what you want to do or who you want to be. You are young and there are so many adventures to enjoy, so many better things to explore. It's called the value of life. And you need to think about it a little more. There are plenty of things that make life valuable.

Just recognize all the present gifts and blessings around you. Forget about what you don't have. Perhaps there is something better for you, waiting for the right season to manifest. And in the end, that will help you to feel happier and live a healthier life.

Ponder on the wisdom of William A. Ward "God gave you a gift of 86,400 seconds today. Have you used one to say "thank you?"

So gratefully, with a smile, say:

"I am grateful for the blessings of my wonderful life. I am thankful for all the blessings I have received in the past, and the blessings I am receiving every moment from my All Mighty God.

What I am today is because of my All Mighty Lord, my Angels, and many other people. Lovingly, with deepest gratitude and a happy heart I give thanks to my Parents, Friends, Teachers and my most Loving Lord, my Guardian Angels and everyone for their nobility and kindness in joy, beauty and light."

Be a Superhero of Encouragement

Discouragement is one of the greatest of human enemies . . . Why are some people able to rise above discouragement?

Because they are able to find the **Superhero of Encouragement** within. They have absolute sublime faith in themselves. Their resolve knows no retreat! They don't listen to negative voices that lead to discouragement during adversity.

Even when they take a backward step, they are confident in their abilities. They don't allow people to discourage them; they choose to face challenges and disappointment head on so they can deal with them directly.

Martin Luther King Jr said "The ultimate measure of a man is not where he stands in moments of comfort and convenience, but where he stands at times of challenge and controversy." This is perfectly true.

A super hero knows how to restore courage when the outlook is bleak. Without courage, we curl up and quit. So dig deep into your **powerhouse of courage**! It's there, waiting to help you take control!

Make each day a real victory! Time is a great healer. Take comfort knowing that everything is temporary! Just as thunderstorms are followed by sunshine, every period of adversity is followed by peace.

Hold your head up, trust your intuition . . . and during adversity, tell yourself . . . *"I am the child of the Most High . . . I am here to express my life fully and enjoy peace and happiness! I am one with God and I trust in God to guide me. My courage is strong and I will prevail as I have the power!"*

Joy Time, Chill out Time in the Present Moment

The very basic nature of the Universe is harmony and serenity. Birds, fishes, and animals instinctively live in harmony with their existence, and even little children want to enjoy all the time, oblivious of the surroundings, in their pristine state of mind.

Animals and little children have the gift of living for the moment. Not only does this bring you greater joy in the moment, it can actually help boost your productivity and efficiency!

American lecturer Ralph Waldo Emerson said "No great work is ever accomplished without joy. Joy stimulates man's inner powers for success and releases them to work for him and through him."

Have you ever said these things?

❖ *I will be able to relax when I achieve certain grades in my studies.*
❖ *I will be happy only when I finally complete my university degree.*
❖ *I will be able to live peacefully once I have a bigger house and a better car.*
❖ *I will be free to enjoy my life when I earn double the amount of money than right now.*

If yes, then it means that your focus is on the future rather than the present and your pursuit of joy is conditional. Such a conditional belief system only makes one spend their entire life chasing joy and happiness, but never receiving it.

In reality, joy and happiness is within us and are not payment for any specific achievement. Work for the future but live joyfully in the present. The only time you are completely in control of your happiness is in the current moment. If you want to be happy, be happy now!

Your life is a gift: experience joy and enjoy chilling out as part of your student-life, teenage life, work life and home life. Haven't we all heard the famous maxim, "*All work and no play makes Jack a dull boy*"?

Avoid Being Dragged Down by Past Experiences

We have all had our share of unpleasant experiences in the past. Sometimes you may feel bogged down by painful experiences from your past. At such times, you must look into your soul and remind yourself that past experiences are your stepping stones to success.

Teacher of Vipassana Meditation, S.N. Goenka once said "One has to live in the present. Whatever is past is gone beyond recall; whatever is future remains beyond one's reach, until it becomes present. Remembering the past and giving thought to the future are important, but only to the extent that helps one deal with the present." So true!

When you make the present moment your priority, your life will become rich and worthwhile not only for yourself, but for all those around you. These positive feelings are contagious and transmit positive vibrations to everyone around you.

Seriously ponder on this wise quote by Oscar Wilde Author and Poet (1854-1900). "A man who is master of himself can end a sorrow as he can invent a pleasure. I don't want to be at the mercy of my emotions. I want to use them, to enjoy them, and to dominate them."

So! Ask yourself, "What can I do to change my present situation?"

Then joyfully decree:

"I focus on the present moment, as it is a gift from my Divine God. No matter where I am or what I am doing, nothing is more important than being happy right now.

I look for all situations to be happy. My happiness is in my present moment. Everything that I have is a divine gift from the Divine Universe. My past was a learning experience. I only remember the good and happy past.

I am happy in my present reality and I now focus on my blessings of the present. I have nothing to worry about the future, as my future is beautiful and I send divine light and divine love to my future."

CHAPTER 4

BE A ROLE MODEL OF GOOD HABITS AND GOOD MORALS

"There is a need for more role models and leaders who are examples of positive authority."

An Orin Book by Sanaya Roman—Living with Joy.

BE A ROLE MODEL OF GOOD HABITS AND GOOD MORALS

Developing Good Habits and Good Morals

*M*orals are the ability to know right and wrong. When we know right and wrong, our decisions become a lot simpler and the consequences are much easier to deal with.

Morals can play a massive part in maintaining health and happiness while achieving success.

Some decisions might not seem like moral issues unless you consider how they will affect your health or long-term well-being. You have a moral responsibility to stay healthy and confident, while some poor decisions may lead to habits that could undermine your health and confidence, even if they seem like harmless fun in the beginning.

Have you ever wondered how some of your habits could affect your life?

While morals represent the right way to make decisions, habits represent the way that we actually *do* them. Everyone has good habits and bad habits. We need to monitor our habits; in case bad habits become so frequent they can damage our health and confidence.

It is also possible to consciously develop good habits that will help us stay healthy and happy.

In a way, habits are like Superheroes and Villains rolled up into one; they can be our best friend and our worst enemy at the same time.

When you have low self-esteem, you turn to other people to give you approval and validate your decisions. It is easier to go along with whatever others are doing when you don't have the confidence to think for yourself. You may pick up some bad habits that will stay alongside you.

When you have a healthy self-esteem, you have confidence in your own ability so you are free to make sensible decisions.

Stay away from negative peer pressure

When your friends push you into a certain pattern of behaviour, this is known as "peer pressure". Peer pressure can be positive or negative.

If your friends recognize the health risks of drugs, cigarettes, and alcohol but still pressure you to experiment with them then you are under negative peer pressure.

If you find yourself doing things that secretly bother you or make you feel uncomfortable or unsafe, then you need to seriously consider finding new friends. So start by developing new interests and hobbies—this will give you a new circle of friends who will support your personal interests.

Good friends support your interests and ambitions, and see your natural talents even when you can't recognize what you are best at. *Such friends will "pressure" you to be your best at whatever you do best—so look out for positive peers like these.*

Be a Good Role Model to Others

Bad Habits are the smooth criminals that slip in unnoticed to sabotage your lifestyle. It is because you don't notice your own bad habits, that they are so dangerous.

So, let's look at a few common and well-known bad habits, so you have a better chance to avoid the damage they can cause.

No Smoking Please

Nobody enjoys smoking the first time they try it. You are drawing toxic smoke into your lungs—who wants to do that?! But there is still an idea among some teenagers that smoking is "cool" and this idea is almost as contagious as smoking itself.

Some of your friends are smoking while you fiddle with your empty hands feeling awkward, and you start to think the smell of smoke in the air isn't so bad. Then you splutter and persevere over your first cigarette in private until you know how to do it right. Once you're old enough not to care about the cool crowd any more . . . you can't stop smoking as it has already become a habit.

It is widely known that smoking damages your health; all the toxic smoke drawing directly into your lungs prevents your lungs from working effectively. Eventually, the toxins can trigger cancer and mess with your ability to breathe.

How do you prevent yourself from smoking when your friends are doing it?

Be a good role model. Advocate "**No Smoking**" Habit.

No Way! No Drugs!

There are many different types of drugs out there. Drugs are deadly, could damage your brain permanently.

Drugs are designed to be entirely addictive—they change your metabolism so powerfully, that you will never feel "normal" again unless you are on the drug. Addicts need higher and higher doses of the drug to feel "normal" but the drug will damage your organs and poison your blood stream.

Why waste money on things that do not bring you happiness. Happiness is your birthright.

Drugs are a waste of time. They are destroyers of our happiness.

Be a Good Role Model, advocate "No Drugs"

No Alcohol Please—My Body is not ready

It is easy to slip into unhealthy habits with alcohol. Each time you drink alcohol, you are burning off your brain cells. Excessive alcohol can damage the liver over time; it can affect your vision and your ability to make good decisions. And it can become addictive.

American author Neale Donald Walsh in his book *Conversation with God* — Book 1 said "If you've ever taken alcohol into your body, you have very little will to live. The body was not meant to intake alcohol. It impairs the mind."

As a teenager, your body is not developed enough yet to process even small levels of alcohol. And your mind is not developed enough to know how to behave when you are under the influence of alcohol. The best decision is to simply **avoid even trying a sip of alcohol.**

How Bad Habits affect others

Have you ever considered how one person's bad habits can affect others? Your habits can affect your friends, your family, and anyone that you are near. For example, when you smoke at the school bus-stop, you are forcing your friends to breathe in your second-hand smoke. You are setting a bad example to younger children.

If you do drugs at home when your parents are at work, then who is watching your younger brothers or sisters? What happens if the police come to the door, and they suspect there are drugs in the premises?

What happens when your younger brother or sister tries drugs for the first time because they saw you doing them, and thought it was okay?

What happens if you drink alcohol until you can't think straight and you insist on driving and hit someone with your car because you didn't see them walking on the road?

All these bad habits have major consequences. You may not think of the wrong that can come out of them in the beginning. Realize that every action has a reaction. Every cause has an effect, and every habit has a consequence. Sometimes a bad habit that seems minor can have major catastrophic consequences.

Many people see your habits before they see you. This includes your younger siblings, neighbours or the new person at school. *You should strive to always be a **good role model** by making smart and good choices.*

Powerful Question!
Is Your Body ready for Sex?

Just like smoking, drinking, or taking drugs, there are also dangers to having sex too early in your life. Sex is often misunderstood and abused. Let's face it; you're barely old enough to understand Algebra and Advanced English Literature. How can you possibly understand something as complex as "sex"?

The truth is that until you are physically mature, your body is not ready for sex. Just as importantly, you are not yet emotionally mature so your sexual relationship is not likely to last as long.

You will find it more difficult to handle all the complications of sex—the need to discuss contraception, the importance of strong communication, and the added heartbreak when the relationship ends.

And you are putting yourself at risk of diseases such as sexually transmitted deadly diseases that are difficult to cure such as: Chlamydia, Crabs, Hepatitis (B and C), Herpes, Syphilis, H.I.V. and AIDS.

There is also the risk of unplanned pregnancy. Having a baby is not only hard work, it is life changing and it lasts a lifetime. While you care for a small child, your own personal development is on hold.

Your teenage years are a time to **grow and learn and become strong and confident** *. . . later you will be a better and happier parent with more to share and give to your own children.*

Making Good Habits

Motivational Speaker Sean Covey said "Depending on what they are, our habits will either make us or break us. We become what we repeatedly do." You have so many good and healthy habits that keep you strong and happy each day without even thinking about it. Each of these habits not only keeps your body in good shape, but also helps you live a happy life.

So what are good habits?

- ❖ *Eating healthy food in moderation to keep you physically strong and healthy.*
- ❖ *Organizing your time effectively.*
- ❖ *Being prudent with money.*
- ❖ *Avoiding drugs and alcohol.*

If you want to enjoy a greater sense of happiness, then you should begin by practicing good habits. After all, the self-discipline of good habits will give you extra time and energy to enjoy greater health and happiness.

Last Minute Syndrome

Perhaps you are a student who tends to do your homework at the very last minute. This is nothing new; it's just how you like to operate. You have a 3-page essay due during your second class. No problem! You'll just do it on the bus, or during your first class.

You have a 10-page term paper due in three days, and you haven't even started. No problem, right! You can just skim your notes, throw something together and hope for a passing grade!

If this is how you operate, then you are doing it all wrong. You may think that this type of bad habit is taking the easy way out. Actually, you are making life harder for yourself. You are also adding unnecessary stress to your life.

Almost all your habits will be developed during your teenage years and they will set the pattern for the rest of your life. And we can assure you that the habit of "waiting until the last minute" will continue to be extremely damaging now and in the future.

Maybe you think: "I'm making so much extra time for myself by waiting until the last minute." Or perhaps you're thinking "I don't really care that much . . . So as long as I get it done, it doesn't matter."

But when you are older and you want to buy a nice car, you will need money. And to get money, you will need a job. And to get a job, you will need to be valuable enough for someone to hire you. Who in their right mind would want to hire someone that waits until the last minute to do everything?

Who wants an employee who always shows up to work late because you waited until the last minute to leave for work, without considering how the morning traffic would affect you. You would wait until the last minute to make phone calls to your clients, and then fail to complete the job when you "just missed" talking to the client. When your boss starts seeing you as inefficient, you will see how this "last minute" habit is affecting your career.

So! If you are the type of person that usually has bad habits, now is the time to address them. Now is the time to change your ways and start practicing good habits.

Fun Challenge! If you are worried that your bad habits are undermining your health or happiness, set yourself a 7 day challenge to break that dangerous habit. Even if you think your life is on track, you could still choose one of the following challenges for 7 days and see how it transforms your life.

Learn how to knit, crochet, do needlework or construct small woodworking kits or model cars or planes: Challenge yourself to learn the skill and create one small hand-made item within 7 days. This challenge will not only give you a new skill and the opportunity to create hand-made gifts for family and friends, it will also keep your hands busy while you are alone or watching the television. So this is a great challenge for those who want to cut down on between-meal snacks or excessive online time. And if you decide after 7 days that you loathe this new skill, at least you don't ever have to do it again after completing the challenge!

How many 1,000 piece jigsaw puzzles can I complete in 7 days? Again, this will keep you occupied during quiet times. Jigsaw puzzles can be soothing while requiring a high level of concentration, and there is always the temptation to fit in one more pieces!

Walk for 30 minutes every day: While some forms of exercise require special equipment and regular appointments, all you need to start walking is decent shoes and the motivation to step out the front door and *go!* You need to complete the walk every day for 7 days, so think ahead about bad weather or busy times, so you don't have excuses to skip your walk. Keep a record of your progress—you might discover that you can walk further than you did on Day 1; and you might also find your brain is sharper and you have better concentration and a healthier appetite. You might prefer the challenge of running or swimming—it's up to you.

Keep a "Happy Diary" for 7 days: Keep a record of the beautiful things you see or the compliments you receive, and the small pleasures and achievements you notch up over 7 days. Don't include worries or arguments or negative upsetting incidents—at the end of 7 days, you will have a clearer sense of what makes you happy.

This is a great challenge for anyone feeling doubts about their identity or ability by focussing on the positives, you have a better sense of what is important to you; and by eliminating negative distressing incidents from your diary, you can pinpoint who or what is dragging you down in real life.

Eat only home-cooked food for 7 days: This doesn't mean you are forced to cook an elaborate 3-course meal three times a day. It simply means you can't rely on restaurants, cafés or takeaways to provide you with ready-made food. It also eliminates packet food such as chips or biscuits—if you want these delicacies, you will need to learn how to cook them yourself! If your cooking time is limited, there is nothing wrong with toast for breakfast and a sandwich for lunch, along with some fruit to fill in the gaps when you are hungry.

When you crave snacks, muffins or cupcakes aren't so bad when you eat them in moderation; and you are more likely to eat in moderation when you know how long it took to prepare them yourself, rather than choosing one off the shelf at the local shop. At the end of 7 days, you will feel healthier; you'll have a greater appreciation of food.

Smile and affirm the following:

"When I make good choices and do things which are good for my health over and over for several days, they become good habits which benefit my mind and body. I feel good about that. I know God made my body special and I want to keep myself healthy and in the best shape I can be."

Shine with Personal Responsibility

Life's lessons are often challenging—and the most challenging lesson is to accept responsibility.

Some people blame others for their failures and unhappiness. They shrug off responsibility by saying: 'It's not my fault'. One problem with this attitude is that they don't learn from their mistakes.

When you say it's not your fault, you have no incentive to improve so there will be countless incidents throughout your life that are "not your fault". As the creator of your own life, you cannot blame others for your blunders or failures. Mistakes are life's most effective learning tool. So acknowledge your mistakes and ask yourself:

❖ *What can I learn from this?*
❖ *How can I avoid this painful situation in the future?*
❖ *How did I set this situation into motion?*

You have the option to consciously design your life as if it was a work of art—shaping it and perfecting it until it is strong and beautiful; or you can blunder repeatedly through the same mistakes. Blame no one for your failures, miseries, crisis, and unhappiness.

It's easy to feel sorry for ourselves when things are tough. But when we find the courage to take responsibility, we are flooded with emotions from relief to liberation.

This is when you can say to yourself, **"Look at what I created! I did this all by myself."** And you will follow positive and empowering thought patterns to create a beautiful life.

Sometimes our flaws are simply poor organizational skills that can undermine our ability to achieve. Acknowledge these flaws and work on finding ways to change.

If you're disorganized, experiment with different organizational tools such as **"To Do"** lists or daily tasks and strict deadlines. If you are a procrastinator, examine your motivation for avoiding important tasks. People usually procrastinate because they are either lacking in confidence, or they really dislike the particular task.

Taking responsibility for everything in your life builds your inner power and begins changing your thoughts to those that serve your higher interest. Taking responsibility for what you think, say and do, will provide you with unlimited strength, confidence and fulfilment.

Smile and Say:

"God gave me this life, but I am the creator of my own happiness. I am the one who is responsible for all my actions. By taking responsibility, I will learn from my mistakes and make changes to improve from these mistakes. By taking responsibility, I will grow into the person I want to be and the person God put me on earth to be."

Be a world class Teenager of Integrity

Author Sean Covey, in his book *7 Habits of Highly Effective Teenagers* said "Stop, take a moment right now and ask: Is the life I'm living leading me in the right direction?"

You reap what you sow. Sow good and beautiful things. Sow love, mercy, kindness, patience, and steadfastness. Do not lie, cheat, and steal to get ahead or your spirit will be devoid of real life. You will be miserable as you lay your head down at night with misery that can only come from such unethical behaviour.

Be brutally honest as you pause and listen to your inner voice, also known as your conscience. What is it telling you? Ask yourself: are you living a life of integrity? If not, change the pattern of your life.

With a warm smile say:

"I have the power. I choose not to give into thoughts of fear and discouragement. I choose to have thoughts of success and happiness. I also choose to create my success with integrity. When I close my eyes at night, I can know I did my best to follow the path God wants me on."

CHAPTER 5

YOUR BODY IS A GIFT. BE SUPERFIT WITH HEALTHY EATING

"To keep the body in good health is a duty . . . otherwise we shall not be able to keep our mind strong and clear."

Buddha

YOUR BODY IS A GIFT
BE SUPERFIT
WITH HEALTHY EATING

You Are What You Eat

Most Prolific Inventor Thomas Edison perfectly pointed that "The doctor of the future will give no medicine, but will interest his patients in the care of the human frame, in diet and in the cause and prevention of disease."

Good eating habits are the key to great health and a happy, lengthy life. In this beautiful universe, there are so many foods readily available it can be difficult to remember the three key rules of healthy eating such as eating in moderation, eating a variety of fresh nutrient-rich food and avoiding fatty, processed food.

Compare your body to a car. If you put the wrong fuel in a car, it will sputter and eventually shut down. It will not work properly. Humans are pretty much the same. Sure, the damage caused by junk food and tasty treats may not show up right away. But over the course of time, too many fatty, heavy and sugary foods will clog up our insides, making us feel tired and heavy.

Think about how we fuel a car. We give it petrol. We fill it up until the belly is full, and it's ready to go. It's that simple. The car knows how to do the rest. Once it is fuelled up, your car is ready to do its magic.

Your body is also a magnificent machine that can always find creative ways to get from point "A to B" while surviving almost all of the elements. With the right nutrient, you will be able to keep moving, and your body and mind will work to the best of their ability and you will be able to reach your full potential.

Build a Super Immune System

Have you ever noticed that some of your class mates seem to be sick and missing class all the time? Check to see what they are eating; I bet they are not eating healthy. Poor eating habits directly affect the strength of our immune system. And it probably explains why they are missing so many classes.

A balanced diet is the foundation of a strong immune system. And nature provides incredibly the best nutritious food to strengthen and support your immune system.

Simply adding more fruits, dairy, vegetables, and grains to your daily diet can improve your immune system greatly. All these foods contain vitamins and minerals that work together to balance our health and protect us from illness.

If you get into the following routines, you can build a super immune system:

Eat 5 portions of fruit and vegetables: Be creative. Slice them, dice them, blend them, steam them or bake them. So long as you are incorporating fruits and veggies into your daily diet who cares how you prepare them!

Eat Oily Fish: Eating fish very often will help boost your memory and concentration. Salmon, mackerel and sardines are great sources of healthy fish oils.

Stay Hydrated: When you don't drink enough fluids, you can actually cause a lot of damage to your body. Stay hydrated (and we do not mean sugary beverages or drinks). Water is always the best option: zero calories and 100% hydration.

Don't Skip Breakfast: Breakfast *is* the most important meal of the day. It starts you off with the energy that you need to get going and *keep* going. Your breakfast sets the tone for your energy levels throughout the rest of your day; it sets the pattern for the way you will eat the rest of the day.

Eat Food With Whole grains: Sneak some extra whole grains into your daily diet. Whole grains are a great way to get healthier, and they are more available than ever, in improved pasta, bread, and products and will help you feel fuller longer.

How to Make Nutrients Do All the Work

You are probably thinking: "So I need carbohydrates, proteins, vitamins, minerals . . . blah blah blah . . . but what do they do, and why do I need them?" Each nutrient is important. They help you have a balanced diet. This allows your body to work better. In normal terms, it will help you sleep better, have more energy, and prevent sickness. Here is a quick breakdown of different nutrients:

Vitamins—Vitamins are a staple of every balanced diet. Each vitamin has its own job to keep you strong and help your body function at optimum capacity. For example, Vitamin A develops your night vision, helping your eyes adjust in the dark. Vitamin C helps you fight disease and infection, while Vitamin D strengthens your bones.

Minerals—Minerals are nutrients that replenish the physical elements of our body: our bones, muscle, nerves and skin. For example, potassium helps your brain send messages to the rest of your body, and calcium strengthens your bones. Every fresh food contains some balance of minerals, so it is vital to eat a variety of foods. Minerals are burnt off when you are active, so you need to replace these resources regularly.

Protein—Protein feeds and builds our muscles, and contributes to our level of energy and strength. Also it is responsible for repairing our cells when we are injured or weak. It is found mostly in meat, but can also be found in certain beans and nuts.

Carbohydrates—Our bodies are mostly made up of carbohydrates. We need this nutrient mostly for energy. And since we are constantly burning energy, we always need to eat carbohydrates. Carbohydrates are found in foods such as bread, potatoes, rice and pasta.

Sugar—Always a tricky one, sugar is a nutrient that directly affects our energy level. Eating the right amounts of sugar can be good for us. Too much sugar can cause severe health problems such as diabetes. It is best to consume natural sugars such as molasses, honey, sorghum, agave nectar, palm sugar, cane sugar, stevia, maple syrup. *Many tasty fruits contain natural sugar also.*

Healthy Fats—While our bodies are designed in a way that they need fat, we should still focus on taking in the right kind of fat. Otherwise, bad fat can lead to heart problems and other issues that are related to being overweight.

To Diet Or Not To Diet, That Is The Question . . .

If you are gaining weight for no healthy reason you need to adjust your daily diet, to minimise "extra" foods that might be providing excess bad calories you struggle to burn off.

Some people assume that "diets" are drastic eating plans to drop weight. But when you cut out a whole food group, you are in danger of starving your body of vital nutrients. Food is not to blame. Maybe you just need to watch how much you eat, when you eat and what you eat.

Right Calorie Diet—Going on a right amount of calorie diet could be a good thing. It can make sure you focus on having a balanced diet.

This is a good start for the healthiest results, make sure that you know exactly how many nutrients you need each day to ensure you stay healthy—otherwise you become malnourished. Eating the right amount of calories combined with doing exercise will help you lose weight.

But always consult a doctor or a nutritionist before drastically changing your daily diet. Otherwise you might actually make matters worse for yourself by damaging your body and undermining your health.

Have a doctor measure your body fat or use a scale that measures your Body Mass Index (a comparison of your weight with your height). This will show you whether you have a healthy weight for your height. If you are underweight or overweight, your doctor can discuss your daily eating pattern and you might discover which eating habit is causing the problem.

"I'm Skinny":
The Little-Discussed Opposite of Being Overweight

Everything has an opposite. The opposite of being overweight is being *underweight*. You might think "Well, if I'm underweight, it means that I am not fat, and that's good." But once you pass a certain point, being underweight can actually be considered a symptom.

You can become malnourished if you are not eating all the nutrients that you need. When you are a teenager, you might feel so much pressure to look good, and be as thin as possible.

Anorexia

Anorexia is where you view yourself as an overweight person even when you are very thin. People with anorexia tend to go on very extreme diets where they limit their food intake close to the point of starvation. Gradually your skin becomes bad, your bones will become brittle and you will have spells of dizziness and fainting. Anorexia can also affect your heart, so it is an extremely dangerous disorder.

Bulimia

Bulimia is an eating disorder where you binge—eat a lot in a small amount of time—on food, and then force yourself to get the food out of your body before you can digest it properly. This is done by vomiting or taking medication to flush the food out of your body before it is digested.

The constant vomiting will damage your teeth as stomach acid breaks down the enamel that keeps your teeth white. You will also become dehydrated from losing fluid, and you could become ill very quickly due to lack of nutrients.

Binge Eating

You cannot tell by a person's weight whether they have an eating disorder. And there are other disorders beside anorexia and bulimia.

If you regularly binge-eat, even without trying to get the food out of your system as a bulimic would, then you might have an eating disorder. You will become excessively overweight and suffer a range of health problems if you do not get your eating habits into a healthier pattern.

There are many factors that cause a person to binge eat, but the main one is a lack of self-control around food. Binge eaters suffer from very different symptoms than those with Anorexia or Bulimia. They feel ashamed about their eating habits and probably find it necessary to eat in secret. They feel a compulsive need to eat but are very worried and embarrassed about how people will react to their binge eating.

Ironically, if you keep your unhealthy habits a secret; you are more likely to develop a serious problem because you are preventing your friends and family from monitoring your behaviour.

Some people binge eat because they are bored. Maybe they get home from school or college and don't have anywhere to go or anyone to call, so they make an ice cream sundae or eat an entire bag of potato chips. The point is that binge eating means that you are eating when you don't need to eat. Binge eating can have obvious effects on your health: foods high in saturated fat will make you gain weight quickly and will put a strain on your heart and vital organs.

Start by making wiser and more nutritious choices, and always ask yourself: *"Am I actually hungry, or do I just want to eat?"*

If you try to make better choices, you will often succeed.

Most of us do not pay attention to these things. We eat for the sake of eating, and never stop to think about *why* we are eating, or how nourishment is important for stronger bones, a healthy heart, and stronger muscles. We eat and drink without considering what we are putting in our bodies. We gulp and swallow because it is tasty, spicy and juicy and never stop to think if it contains a lot of sugar, or fat. You just need to make better decisions and treat yourself better. It is important and will affect the way that you feel, and the way that your body feels.

With a smile say to yourself:

"From now on I will pay more attention to what I eat and drink for the sake of my good health and prevention of illnesses.

I will make wiser nutritious choices. I will bless my food with love and gratitude and eat my food with a grateful heart."

CHAPTER 6

GET GREAT IN THE LEARNING RELEARNING AGE

"Anyone who stops learning is old, whether at twenty or eighty. Anyone who keeps learning stays young."

Henry Ford

GET GREAT IN THE LEARNING RELEARNING AGE

Era of the Information Revolution

A futurist writer well-known for corporate revolution, Alvin Toffler, in his book *The Third Wave*, described the present era as an information revolution and that this wave will last forever. "The illiterate of the 21st century will not be those who cannot read and write, but those who cannot learn, unlearn and relearn."

Toffler summed up the explosion of the 'Information and Knowledge' economy simply as the **'Learning and Relearning Age.'**

The learners consistently move forward because of their scope of knowledge, willingness to update themselves with the latest knowledge, and most importantly, because of their ability to apply that knowledge.

As a student you have learned and gained knowledge in the classroom. This is great, but the most important part is what are you going to do with this knowledge outside of the classroom? How can you take the knowledge and make a positive impact on your life?

Your Life's Journey is a School

Author Sanaya Roman in her book *Personal Power through Awareness* gave an impressive piece of wisdom, "Growth never ends; forever when you reach higher levels there are still further levels to go. Without growth there is a contraction of life-force energy. With growth you feel vibrant, alive, healthy and joyful."

There is always something new to learn. Thinking you have mastered something completely is an illusion leading to stagnation. Everywhere you go there is something new to learn or a new way to look at an issue. By making yourself believe THAT you are going to learn something new every day, whether you are in the classroom or not, is a great way to keep your mind sharp and taking in all that life has to offer.

As the Zen masters say, keep a **"beginner's mind"** and keep expanding your knowledge with curiosity and delight. The more you learn, the more you expand your horizons.

Be a liberal learner of the world. With vast knowledge, you seize many opportunities.

Do not get trapped in the world of complacency and ignorance; otherwise, you will get left behind. Always be looking for new things to learn. ***Knowledge is power***.

Upgrade the quality of your thinking by developing an intellectual, productive, creative and inquisitive mind, which will enable you to adapt to the continually changing environment.

This life's journey is a school. You are here to learn, improve, and grow. Learning develops mental faculties, sharpens skills and creates self-improvement in this ever-changing world. Furthermore, it opens opportunities for lucrative employment, creates a sense of independence, builds self-confidence, boosts your competitiveness in the global marketplace and contributes to the sustainable economic growth of your country.

Most beneficial of all, it enhances **character excellence** and takes you to the **league of super riches**. This leads to a more evolved society intellectually, emotionally and spiritually. It also adds **immeasurable goodness to our Divine Universe**.

With a smile, say to yourself:

"I will keep learning what I don't know. I will approach learning with the boundless enthusiasm of a child who is eager to learn about everything. I will embrace lifelong learning as an enjoyable quest."

CHAPTER 7

BE EXTRAORDINARY WITH MISSIONS AND GOALS

"You control your future, your destiny. What you think about comes about. By recording your dreams and goals on paper you set the motion in process of becoming the person you want to be. Put your future in good hands—your own hands."

Mark Victor Hansen

BE EXTRAORDINARY
WITH MISSIONS
AND GOALS

Magical Powers of Written Goals

*W*riting goals down is like creating a blue print of what you wish to achieve in life. Otherwise goals in your mind remain as unachievable dreams.

Robin Sharma in his book *Be Extraordinary* said "Setting your goals is a bold play for your best life. Setting your goals is an act of heroism because you are reaching for the potential that has been invested in you." Great statement!

Written goals have some magical powers: they create desire and enthusiasm. You will feel the increase in energy, enthusiasm and the burning desire to achieve the goals becomes stronger and this leads to have an action **PLAN.**

Also writing forces us to **THINK.** The more we think, the more we challenge our idle brain cells to find an answer to the next question. How can I make that happen?

Marc Allen the author of *The Millionaire Course* shared this phrase "The single most important thing your written plan does is remind your powerful subconscious mind that you desire this, and you focus on that desire by putting it in concrete words on paper so your subconscious can get to work on it." Perfect Wisdom!

Build your Success with Great Goals

Ask yourself what you aspire to achieve during this phase of your life. What do you want to achieve within 1 years, 3 years or immediately?

Set broad, forward-looking goals for your education, your career, family, finances, personal achievements and health.

For example you may dream of being fit enough to run a marathon. This is an enormous undertaking, so first you need to set up a goal for the first milestone: to be able to run a certain distance by a certain date. Once you have met this goal, you can set a more challenging goal, so you can run further.

Eventually you will meet the ultimate goal of being able to run a marathon. To achieve your goal you must have a strategy—for example, you need to commit a certain number of hours each week to training—and to meet your commitments, you may have to make sacrifices, such as limiting the time you spend with friends.

Goals Must Have Priorities, Be Specific and Measurable

When you have several goals, rank them according to priority so that you stay focused on the most important ones. Make sure your goals are achievable and the timeline is reasonable. If you set goals that are impossible to reach, you will find yourself getting discouraged.

But your goal-setting plan is only effective when it is very specific and measurable. For example if one of your immediate GOAL is to lose weight about 10 kg in the next three months, and your strategy is to exercise, this is a great goal but not specific, measurable and attainable.

Begin with a small achievable goal—"I want to lose 1 kg in a week". When you meet the goal within the time-frame, you will feel a boost of confidence and greater motivation to achieve a more challenging goal. When you set a goal that is too vague or unrealistic, you will lose your motivation.

Next, examine your present circumstances to check off goals that have been achieved.

Keep a progress record of your goals. By breaking it down into smaller short-term goals, you have the opportunity to regularly tick off the milestone achievements.

Actions or Excuses

Okay you have got all your goals written and the appropriate strategies with the corresponding benefits and the action plan. After writing are you going to just sit around AND do nothing? Will you make excuses or take action?

Here are some of the common excuses used to avoid working towards your goal:

❖ *I am not in the mood, perhaps tomorrow.*

- *I don't have the brains.*
- *Today and tomorrow are not convenient, perhaps the day after.*
- *My friends are waiting so I will postpone doing it. Still got time. Can wait.*
- *There is a good movie now. I will start later.*

Procrastination can hold you back from achieving your goal. You should commit to doing at least one thing every day toward achieving your dream.

"Procrastination robs you of opportunity. It is a significant fact that no great leader was ever known to procrastinate" said Napoleon Hill.

Some people are afraid of failures so they procrastinate. If you are afraid of failing, or if your first attempted strategies don't work, you might be tempted to give up altogether. This is when you need to look around at achievers you admire and ask yourself:

- *Did they ever fail?*
- *What did they do next?*
- *Did they try again?*

The great inventor Thomas Edison did not lose focus on action even though he keeps failing. His capacity of action was on a continuous attempt until he got it right. This capacity of action unfolds numerous inventions to the world. Thomas Edison and many others have left GOLDEN FOOTPRINTS with an overwhelming passion for their goals. Their achievement could not have the pinnacle of success without action.

So! What are you waiting for? **Give yourself a powerful GIFT.** Start writing beautifully what you want to achieve.

With a smile, joyfully say to yourself:

"I radiate divine light to my goals and visions. I now take action with total commitment and imagine its success.

I believe in myself and know I am capable to be a wonderfully successful person.

While working towards my ultimate goals, I celebrate each small step as a victory."

CHAPTER 8

LOVE-LOVE IS YOUR BIRTHRIGHT

"Acknowledging people and acknowledging yourself is another way to experience love. Take a moment to appreciate everyone you see and send them a feeling of love. This will change your life and raise your vibration rapidly."

An Orin Book by Sanaya Roman—Living with Joy

LOVE–LOVE IS YOUR BIRTHRIGHT

Love is the Ultimate Divine Gift

*N*ew thought Author Prentice Mulford (1834-1891) said "Love is an element which though physically unseen is as real as air or water. It is an acting, living, moving force . . . it moves in waves and currents like those of the ocean." Well said.

Love is the natural state of our Divine Universe. It is the pure life force. Love has the most superior power to manifesting happiness. There is nothing that is not blessed with the power of love. Everything in our Divine Universe is created out of love.

*Your presence in this Universe is because **you are loved.***

So! Love begins within you. When you love yourself, others will naturally love you too. **Fall in love with your life; it is a GIFT!**

The purpose of your life is to love every moment, wherever you are for the experience, the gifts it has given you, and for its many wise lessons. Love every part of you; love your hair, love your eyes, and love your hands. Love your mistakes and achievements.

Surround yourself with love every moment of your life. Make every thought, every word, and every action in the vibration of love.

First Law of Love.
Love your Parents: they are sacred gifts

Your parents are subject to the same human frailties as you are, and if you become a parent yourself you will likely realize this. Instead of laying blame for your parents' shortcomings, you should appreciate and celebrate the sacrifices your parents made for you.

Some of us may not know our birth parents or have a relationship with them. These living adoptive parents or guardian parents have stepped in to care for some of us. These parents should also be honoured because they chose you and put you above themselves. Adoptive parents and guardians are sacred gifts from God.

Cherish your parents and tell them you love them. Make an effort to thank them for the sacrifices they made for you. This might be difficult if you are estranged or hold a grudge about something they did. But there is a reason God sent you these unique parents, and when they are gone it will be too late to tell them how much you appreciate the gift of life that they gave you.

Don't wait for special days to pay respect to the people who have raised and cared for you. Don't let the day go by without honouring them. Honouring is a meaningful gesture; an act of gratitude to the people who helped you to become the unique person you are today.

Take the wisdom from Ephesians 6:1.

"Honour your father and mother," which is the first commandment with promise: "that it may be well with you and you may live long on the earth."

See Divinity in Everyone and Everything

Martin Luther King. Jr said "I have decided to stick with Love. Hate is too great a burden to bear."

You will fully agree hate is too great a burden to bear. So love all your friends, love your teachers, and love your siblings. Love the strengths and weaknesses of everyone. **Spread love in times of anger and hatred.**

Take heed of this beautiful wisdom from *Merlin the Magician*

"If you see aspects of yourself that you feel are not very pretty, you love them anyway, heaven knows your beauty grows. Appreciate those aspects of yourself. Depreciation holds little worth.

Love all conditions, for they have brought you to where you are, and they will carry you very far. Where you are is the only place that can take you to where you want to be. You are moving to that glorious state of consciousness that is unconditional love."

See divinity in everyone and everything, and as you do so, you will be flooded with thoughts of love. Live only in the thought of love for all, and you will draw love to you from all.

In every instance where you catch yourself thinking negative and unkind thoughts about someone, replace those thoughts with thoughts of love. You will be surprised to find yourself becoming more joyful, happier and blissful each moment.

With a smile, make a resolution right now and say:

"I will love every moment of my life. I love the feeling of being born into this beautiful divine Universe. I love myself. I love my life.

I love this beautiful Universe. I radiate love to everyone and everything of this divine Universe.

I will always respond with love and undertake all my endeavours with love."

CHAPTER 9

EVERY GIFT OF KINDNESS IS AN ACT OF HEROISM

"The real point is that we all need help somewhere along life's path whether we think we will or not.

And, if you are the one giving and helping, just remember this: no matter what happens later, you will always be secure in the fact knowing that you have remained strong and true to assist those that need your help."

Catherine Pulsifer

EVERY GIFT OF KINDNESS IS AN ACT OF HEROISM

What You Give is What You Get

*A*uthor Napoleon Hill in his book *Law of Success* wisely penned this related wisdom "There can never be success without happiness, and no man can be happy without dispensing happiness to others."

Just think about the last time you were down—didn't you wish someone would have been there to help you through the tough times?

Or do you remember ever being surprised by someone—a friend or a relative—who brought you a gift just to show that they care?

Helping other people discover happiness is a great source of personal satisfaction. Unselfishness is a warm and perpetuating gift: when you perform an act of **KINDNESS** to make others feel better. It could be as simple as giving delicious meals and clothes to homeless people, or by taking out the garbage for your parents without being asked.

What these all have in common is that they will bring a smile to someone's face or brighten up someone's otherwise "bad day". And you will feel better about yourself and have a greater perspective to your own challenges.

Rather than brooding on your own problems, open your mind to others and consider how their problems compare to yours.

Every seed you scatter offers the promise of millions of fruits. The purpose of kindness is to **bring happiness to others** and in turn you receive happiness and fulfillment.

Some people might think they have nothing to contribute to those in need. Yet some of the most inspiring and generous people in history came from humble circumstances. Rather than dwelling on their own deprivations, **they seek to benefit others.**

Mother Teresa, for example, was born to a very poor family in Macedonia. When little Teresa's father died, her mother struggled to raise a young family in dire circumstances. Despite their grim poverty, Teresa's mother always invited others to share their humble meal.

Mother Teresa grew up understanding the law of kindness from early childhood and she is now a legendary icon of philanthropy and an inspiration to generations. She dedicated her life to the mission of being kind to others. Establishing her "Missionary of Charities" throughout the world to continue her legacy beyond her lifetime. Mother Teresa proclaimed *that when we make others' lives worthwhile, our lives become worthwhile.*

You may think you have nothing to give, yet there are so many souls craving for some nurturing or nourishment. You can help a neglected hungry animal. Contribute your time to a philanthropic organization. Delight a sick or lonely person with some flowers.

Listen when someone needs to talk through their problems; speak soothingly to those who are distressed; offer a meal to the man begging on the street; spend time with the lonely; and distribute honest compliments freely.

Motivational Speaker Leo Buscaglia said. "Too often we underestimate the power of a touch, a smile, a kind word, a listening ear, an honest compliment, or the smallest act of caring, all of which have the potential to turn a life around."

Rejoice in the Happiness of others

Do you sometimes feel envious of others who are happy or successful? Do you feel resentful when a friend brags he has achieved something you have dreamed of for yourself as well?

Jealousy and envy are generated from a sense of entitlement and frustration. Behind your friend's success story is a tale of hard work and dedication.

Likes attract likes. If you truly rejoice in the success of others, **you will attract success for yourself.**

But by constantly harbouring negative feelings about others, and wanting their success to dwindle, you drain your own creativity to success. Break free from such feelings as it is detrimental to your own success.

Conversely, when you can rejoice in the good fortune of others, it is a sign that you are confident in your own achievements. Again, this is a self-perpetuating emotion—when you have the confidence to congratulate others, you strengthen your own confidence in your ability to achieve your goals.

With a nice smile declare:

"I rejoice in the success of others. All of humanity deserves to walk in abundance of joy, peace, bliss and happiness. By sharing in the success of others I strengthen my own confidence as well as my empathy. Life is amazing! I love to see people who are happy. The Universe is good to us all! We are all worthy of all the happiness."

The Golden Rule!
Embrace the World as One Family

Embracing the world as one family means **oneness with all humanity**. This sacred principle has been taught in all spiritual literatures of all religions.

Everyone is a noble contributor to this Universe. Every day we serve one another. We are interdependent on one another; like the biological cells in our body system which need one another for support. Without each other's support our body system will collapse. In the same manner we need each others' support.

Reach out to learn about another culture. When you understand some people choose to dress differently or observe their religion differently, you are bridging the gap between cultures. Jimmy Carter once said "We have become not a melting pot but a beautiful mosaic. Different people, different beliefs, different yearnings, different hopes, different dreams." This is truly awesome!

Diversity makes for a rich tapestry. All the threads of the tapestry are equal in value. Cherish, appreciate and respect diversity, culture, religion and race.

Spiritual Author Dr Wayne W. Dyer in his book *Wisdom of the Ages* expressed so beautifully. "Use fewer labels that distinguish you from "them." You are not an American, Californian, Italian, and Jew, middle-aged, stocky, female, athletic, or any other label. You are a citizen of the world, and when you stop the labelling process you will begin to see God in every garden, every forest, every home, every creature, and every person, and inner peace will be your reward."

We are a global society. Everyone is entitled to respect because every human being on earth contributes to the society every moment regardless of their position, status, race, income and social class. Embrace the entire human diversity as one race in this world.

Participate in the festivals of other faiths to savour their culture and heritage wholeheartedly and share the amazing spirit and light of oneness and you will **see the divinity in others.**

Napoleon Hill in his book *Law of Success* said "We are all bound together by common ties. The rich and the poor, the learned and the ignorant, the strong and the weak, are woven together in one social and civic web."

So! Grow in harmony and friendship. Develop a pure heart and mind that cherish all religions, race and culture without bias or partiality. See divinity in everyone and everything, because everyone and everything is the creation of God.

With a warm smile say:

Make a commitment that every moment, wherever you are, whomever you meet, you will bring gifts of kindness in the form of silently saying:

"I will help. I will serve. I will bless. I will reach out and touch others. I will elevate every ordinary moment to a delightful moment.

I will see God in everyone and everything. I will radiate divine light and divine love to everyone and everything in all the Kingdom of God."

CHAPTER 10

THE DIVINE SOURCE OF YOUR LIFE AND YOUR GIFTS

"Everything around you exists as part of the universal mind, also called God/All—That-Is."

Sanaya Roman—Spiritual Growth

THE DIVINE SOURCE
OF YOUR LIFE
AND YOUR GIFTS

The Kingdom of God is the ultimate source of your Happiness

*A*ll the gifts that exist around you are because of our most loving, kind, and all-mighty Divine God. Our Divine God is our provider and the original source of all the things that are given to you and are being given to you and will be given to you.

Keep your loving Divine God in your mind, in every thought, every act and in whatever endeavour you undertake. Communicate with your Divine God about all your heart's desires. As the spiritual saying goes, **"first seek the Kingdom of God"** as the Kingdom of God is the source of your happiness. Pour out all of your heart's desires and needs to God.

Spiritual Author Dr Wayne W. Dyer in his book *Wisdom of the Ages* said "Express your wishes in the form of a request to your name or phrase for the creative intelligence that many call, God. Be willing to ask for help and don't be embarrassed to put your request in writing as well as voicing it. "Ask and you shall receive" is not an empty promise." So true!

Prayers—The Ultimate Bridge to Happiness

Alfred, Lord Tennyson said, "More things are wrought by prayer than this world dreams of."

Robert Collier penned wisely in his famous book *Prayer Works!* "Our whole life should be a life of prayer. We should walk in constant communion with God. There should be a constant upward looking of the soul to God. We should walk so habitually in his presence that even when we awake in the night it would be the most natural thing in the world for us to speak to Him in thanksgiving or in petition."

Prayer is the ultimate bridge to happiness. Even if formal prayer is not part of your everyday routine, you will still be compelled to pray sometimes—either giving thanks for the blessings in your life, or asking for support and guidance for an overwhelming problem.

You may see some students praying before they eat their lunch. You may witness athletes praying before they take the field in hopes that it will protect them and their team-mates from getting injured during the game. And most commonly, you may see other students praying before they take a major exam because they really don't want to fail.

When you pray, an incredible amount of positive energy is received. This energy goes into giving you the strength and serenity to overcome challenging situations. Prayer can help you handle all the stress that you encounter at home, at school and among your friends. Prayer can help clear your mind so you can focus on solving your problems.

No matter how and when you call upon this most kind, loving power, it will respond to you. Whatever you are undertaking, know that your loving God is with you, guiding you and protecting you.

This is history's most famous prayer by St. Francis of Assisi (1182-1226). Reciting this prayer will help you keep a healthy perspective and will develop a greater appreciation for your blessings in life.

Lord, make me a channel of thy peace;

That where there is hatred, I may bring love;
That where there is wrong, I may bring the spirit of forgiveness;
That where there is discord, I may bring harmony;
That where there is error, I may bring truth;
That where there is doubt, I may bring faith;
That where there is despair, I may bring hope;
That where there are shadows, I may bring light;
That where there is sadness. I may bring joy.

Lord,
Grant that I may seek rather to comfort than to be comforted;
To understand, than to be understood;
To love, than to be loved;
For it is by self-forgetting that one finds;
It is by forgiving that one is forgiven;
It is by dying that one awakens to eternal life.

CONCLUSION

A PLEDGE
Perfect Health and A Promise of Happiness and Success

*N*ow that you have learned many Rockstar principles of perfect health, happiness and success. Make a pledge to yourself.

We have put together this simple but honest Pledge & Promise. Follow this through and be honest with yourself. This is a personal vow designed to motivate you throughout your personal journey. After all, this is for you, and will only help you find happiness and achieve strength and good health in your life. Feel free to modify the pledge to better fit your personal journey. Sign it, hang it up somewhere where you will see it every day, and read it often.

I am a precious child of this beautiful universe. I deserve Perfect Health, Happiness and Success.

I am here to discover myself and experience life's joys while embarking on my personal journey towards fulfillment and success. During my adventures, I will be kind and respectful, and honour, cherish, love and applaud myself and others. I am here to grow intellectually and spiritually, and to become a better version of myself.

I will channel all judgmental thoughts away, and consciously choose thoughts that are joyful, righteous, and happy. I will remove feelings of hatred, anger, fear, jealousy, selfishness and develop love for all humanity.

I will erase negative emotions and move on from negative events to positive events. I will be a role model of all the positive things.

I will turn to my loving GOD in every thought, every act and in whatever endeavour I undertake. I will communicate with God on all my heart's desires.

I am a gift. My life is a gift. I make peace with everyone in every situation, while still remaining true to myself. And I will allow my positive experiences and energy to lead me towards a life of perfect health, happiness and success.

Signature _____

Special Praises, Gratitude and Appreciation

Our sources for the quotes are many and they are gathered from several sources: books, internet, articles, reviews, magazines etc.

We highly praise the following authors' wisdoms, quotes in their books, as they have always inspired us. We recommend all our dear readers these books for a richer and happy life.

References and Suggested Reading:

Books

Alvin Toffler, *The Third Wave* (Bantam Books, 1980).

Andrew Matthews, *Being a Happy Teenager* (Seashell Publishers Australia 2001).

Eckhart Tolle, The *Power of Now* (New World Library, USA, 2005).

Dr. Wayne W. Dyer, *Wisdom of the Ages* (Harper Collins Publishers Inc 1998).

Dr Wayne W. Dyer, *Wishes Fulfilled* (Hay House UK Ltd 2012).

Hill Napoleon, *Law of Success* (Success Unlimited, 1979).

Laurence G. Bold, *The Tao of Abundance* (Penguin Group 1999).

Marelin the Magician, *Merlin's Message* (Serious Comedy Publications 2006).

Marc Allen, *The Millionaire Course* (New World Library 2003).

Mark Victor Hansen & Barbara Nichols & Patty Hansen, *Out of the Blue* (Advantage Quest Publications 1996).

Neale Donald Walsh, *Conversation with God:* Book One (Hodder and Stoughton 1997).

Orin Book by Sanaya Roman, *Living with Joy* (HJ Kramer Inc and New World Library, 2011).

Robin Sharma, *Life's Lessons from the Monk who sold his Ferrari* (Harper Collins Publishers London Ltd 2013).

Robin Sharma, *The Greatness Guide Book* (Simon & Schuster Inc New York 2008).

Robin Sharma, *Be Extraordinary: The Greatness Guide Book Two* (Harper Elements London Ltd 2013).

Ryonda Bryne, *The Power* (Atria Books division of Simon & Schuster Inc USA 2010).

Robert Collier, *Prayer Works* (www.Self-Improvement-ebook.com 2007).

Sean Covey, *7 Habits of Highly Effective Teenagers* (Simon & Schuster UK Ltd 2004).

Sanaya Roman, *Personal Power through Awareness* (HJ Kramer Inc, 1986).

Sanaya Roman, *Spiritual Growth* (HJ Kramer Inc, 1989).

Swami Rama, *The Art of Joyful Living* (Himalayan Institute Press USA 2004).

Walter M. Bortz II MD and Randan Stickrod, *The Road to 100* (Palgrave Macmillan 2010).

Websites

http://en.wikipedia.org/wiki/Mother_Teresa

http://www.americancatholic.org/Features/Francis/peaceprayer.asp